BRITAIN AT WAR
AIR RAIDS

Martin Parsons

WAYLAND

Editor: Jason Hook
Designer: Simon Borrough
Cartoon artwork: Richard Hook

First published in 1999 by Wayland Publishers Ltd, 61 Western Road, Hove, East Sussex, BN3 1JD, England

© Copyright 1999 Wayland Publishers Ltd
Find Wayland on the Internet at http://www.wayland.co.uk

British Library Cataloguing in Publication Data
Parsons, Martin
    Air raids. - (The history detective investigates Britain at War)
    1. World War, 1939-1945 - social aspects - Great Britain -
    Juvenile literature 2. Great Britain - History - George VI,
    1936-1952 - Juvenile literature 3. Great Britain - Social
    conditions - 20th century - Juvenile literature
    I. Title
    941'.084
ISBN 0 7502 2310 3

Printed and bound in Italy by G. Canale & C.S.p.A, Turin
Cover picture: (bottom) a school gas-mask drill at Windsor in 1941; (top-centre) a recruiting poster for the Auxiliary Fire Service; (top-right) an air-raid warden's helmet.
Title page: A London air-raid warden at his post, September 1939.

Picture Acknowledgements: The publishers would like to thank the following for permission to reproduce their pictures: Getty Images *title page*, 11 (bottom), 13 (bottom), 18 (top), 19 (left), 21 (left), 22 (top); Imperial War Museum, London 4 (top), 12 (bottom), 17 (bottom), 25 (bottom), 26, 27 (top); John Frost Historical Newspapers 6 (right); London Transport Museum 27 (bottom); Peter Newark's Historical Pictures *cover* (top-right), 9 (bottom-left), 11 (left), 19 (right); Popperfoto *cover* (bottom), 7 (left), 9 (top), 10 (right), 15 (bottom), 16 (right), 29; Public Record Office 9 (top-left), 14 (left), 19 (bottom), 20 (top), 23, 28 (left); Science and Society Picture Library 4 (bottom), 14 (right), 25 (top), 28 (right); Topham 7 (right), 8, 10 (left), 21 (right); Wayland Picture Library, photography by Rupert Horrox, courtesy of the Imperial War Museum, London *cover* (top-centre), 5, 6 (left, bottom), 11 (top-right), 12 (top), 13 (top), 17 (top), 20 (bottom), 22 (bottom), 24; Wayland Picture Library 16 (left), 18 (bottom). Logo artwork by John Yates.

All Wayland books encourage children to read and help them improve their literacy.

✓ The contents page, page numbers, headings and index help locate specific pieces of information.

✓ The glossary reinforces alphabetic knowledge and extends vocabulary.

✓ The further information section suggests other books dealing with the same subject.

✓ Find out more about how this book is specifically relevant to the National Literacy Strategy on page 30.

CONTENTS

AIR RAIDS

Many photographs we see of Britain during the Second World War show the effects of air raids. Bombs dropped on British cities by German aeroplanes reduced people's homes to rubble. We see broken buildings, buses in bomb craters, people in shelters, and famous landmarks surrounded by smoke. Can you imagine how shocked and frightened people must have been?

Air raids meant that people in Britain were directly involved in the fighting between 1939 and 1945. What was done to protect people? Where did they shelter? What did air-raid wardens do? There are many clues to tell us. By finding these clues, you can discover how people in your local area learnt to survive an air raid.

The picture below was taken during the first air raid on London, 7 September 1940. You can see the smoke billowing over Tower Bridge.

A London bus on the edge of a crater caused by a bomb which landed on Balham Underground station in October 1940.

The history detective Sherlock Bones will help you to find your clues. You should then be able to collect enough evidence and information to present your own project about air raids.

Wherever you see one of Sherlock's paw-prints, like this, you will find a mystery to solve. The answers can all be found on page 31.

The strange object below was invented for pet owners, because people were afraid that bombs containing poisonous gas would be dropped during air raids. What do you think the object might be? (You can find some clues on page 29.)

DETECTIVE WORK

You can find many clues by tracking down your local Record Office. This building contains many important documents about air raids. Try to find the number and address of the Record Office in your local telephone directory. The history detective Sherlock Bones will tell you on the following pages what clues you need to look for when you visit the Record Office.

The shoes below were 'gas proof'. What do you think wore them?

Air Raid Precautions

Before the Second World War began, people knew that German aeroplanes would drop bombs on cities and ports. The Government had to make plans to protect both lives and buildings. Together we will investigate how successful these plans were.

County Councils set up ARP committees. ARP stands for Air Raid Precautions. The notes or 'minutes' written during the meetings of ARP committees can provide us with many clues. They reveal details about air-raid shelters, wardens and the blackout.

On 10 March 1938, the Government sent out two documents, ARP (General Schemes) and ARP (Fire Schemes). You may be able to find them in your local Record Office. These documents told the ARP committees the many things they had to do before war broke out. They began their preparations by organizing teams of ARP workers and wardens.

Badges were important to identify different officials during air raids.

🐾 What different sorts of people do you think might have worn the badges shown on this page?

A.R.P. Springs Into Action

SANDBAG WALLS RISE AND POSTS MANNED

BY A SPECIAL CORRESPONDENT

LONDON put the finishing touches to its A.R.P. yesterday, quickly but without excitement. Warden posts were manned and fire-alarm posts were protected.

The face of London changed in a day. In one district where no work was visible at 10 o'clock, three Warden Posts had sandbag reinforcement six feet high all round their walls before lunch.

As I drove round I saw dozens of fresh painted notices of this sort: "To the trenches," or "First Aid Post."

Girls Fill Sandbags

Hospitals and medical authorities want blood donors: one volunteer undergoing test.

Heavy Penalties

Newspapers like this one from September 1939 were full of headlines and stories about ARP preparations.

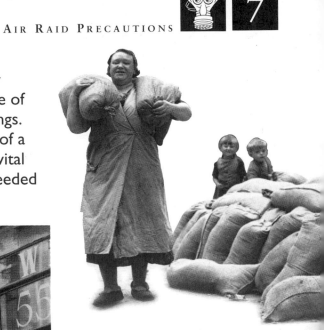

Experts had estimated that 5 per cent of all British property would be destroyed in the first three weeks of air raids. One of the ARP workers' first jobs was to protect important buildings. You might be able to find a photograph in your local library of a building surrounded by sandbags. ARP workers also stored vital equipment, such as the pumps and hoses which would be needed to put out fires caused by incendiary bombs.

Volunteers protect a newspaper office with sandbags.

This lady is busy filling sandbags to protect her home from bomb blasts. The picture was taken on 31 August 1939 just before the war started.

❖ Can you work out where the picture above was taken? You may have to look more carefully than you think.

❖ What do you think is hanging from the right hand of the lady on the right of the photograph?

DETECTIVE WORK

Telephone the Record Office, and ask if you can see the ARP committee minutes from September 1938 to September 1939. When you arrive these documents should be waiting for you. Find out as much as you can about the preparations for air raids in your local area. Make a list of the names of important people. You will come across them many times.

PREPARATIONS

Before the war started, the Government feared that air raids would cause terrible destruction. They sent out thousands of papier-mâché and cardboard coffins. They also believed that 2,800,000 extra hospital beds would be needed. **One of the ARP committees' main tasks was to make plans that would reduce the number of casualties.**

One of the first steps the committees took was to provide air-raid shelters, to protect people from falling bombs. Children were evacuated from cities to safer areas of the country.

Each ARP committee organized its own team of air-raid wardens. Wardens were responsible for giving out air-raid warnings, guiding people to the shelters and organizing emergency services. ARP wardens gave out information to the public, so that they would know where to go when the bombing started.

These women were members of the ARP in Gravesend, Kent.

A warden (right) fits a child with a gas mask known as a Mickey Mouse mask because of its strange appearance.

LOOKOUT IN THE BLACKOUT

UNTIL YOUR EYES
GET USED TO
THE DARKNESS
TAKE IT EASY

This poster advised people to wait until their eyes had adjusted to the dark when stepping into the darkness of the blackout.

There were fears that some bombs would contain poisonous gas. ARP workers gave out gas masks to the public. Wardens were trained to detect poisonous gas, sound warnings with sirens, rattles and bells, and decontaminate affected areas.

ARP committees also organized the 'blackout'. This meant that people were not allowed to use any lights during the hours of darkness, so that cities could not be seen by German pilots. Wardens are best remembered for their role in the blackout, and for always telling people to 'put that light out!'

* Ordinary people gained a lot of power by working for the ARP. Why do you think some other people were upset by this?
* What sort of volunteers are being asked for in Sherlock's newspaper?

DETECTIVE WORK

Visit your local reference library. Ask to use the microfilm viewer to look at local newspapers for 1938–9. Try to track down the reports of ARP planning. Some libraries have microfilm readers which will copy the page you want at the press of a button.

WARDENS – TRAINING

A memo issued by the Government in January 1937 introduced the idea of an air-raid warden service. The memo said: 'An air-raid warden will be a responsible member of the public chosen to be a leader and adviser of his neighbours in a ... small group of streets in which he is known and respected.'

A warden enjoys a cup of tea before he goes on duty.

The poster below was used in 1939 to persuade people to join the ARP.

AIR RAID WARDENS WANTED

A RESPONSIBLE JOB FOR RESPONSIBLE MEN

ARP

APPLY TO YOUR LOCAL COUNCIL NOW

NATIONAL SERVICE

❀ Why do you think this advert might have made people want to become wardens?

Most wardens were volunteers who did the job in their spare time. They were trained in first aid and were sent to anti-gas schools to learn how to deal with bombs containing poison gas. Small communities had to provide their own training for wardens. In the ARP committee minutes, you might find clues as to the type of training your local wardens received.

✤ Compare this poster to the one on page 10. What is different about the words it uses?

The rest of the population was trained as well. Advertisements were placed in local newspapers, warning people of air-raid practices. These practices gave wardens a chance to try out the sirens and rattles they used to alert people, and to rehearse helping people find their way to the shelters.

A warden's helmet and rattle.

A cartoon poster asking people to volunteer as firefighters.

DORSET DAILY ECHO
23 JUNE 1939

A siren test will be carried out in Dorchester on Wednesday June 28 at 10.30 am. A siren will be sounded and will give a warbling note for two minutes and after a minute's interval will give a long blast sounding the all clear.

A mother walking with her baby in an area where there had been a Civil Defence exercise using tear gas.

DETECTIVE WORK

In January 1937, the Government advertised on radio for people to volunteer for warden service. You may be able to track down tapes of the radio broadcasts in the Imperial War Museum. Prepare a list of questions you would ask someone if you were interviewing them for a job as an air-raid warden.

WARDENS—A RAID

The first air raid took place on 7 September 1940 in London. It is difficult for those of us born after the war to imagine what it must have been like. An air raid was incredibly noisy, with bombs exploding, buildings collapsing, fires burning, ambulance bells ringing and people screaming. It was also very smoky, dusty, and – in an area where hoses were putting out fires – very wet!

A plaque like this was put on the outside of a warden's post and sometimes displayed on a warden's house.

AIR RAID WARDEN

In built-up areas, there were wardens' posts which were continually manned during air raids. The role of the wardens was very important and very dangerous. They had to make sure that all homes had their blackout curtains in place, and that no lights were showing. They guided people to shelters, and tried to ensure that people remained calm.

It cannot have been easy to stop people panicking. Bombs were falling from the sky, along with shrapnel from the anti-aircraft guns and debris from damaged buildings.

This is a famous picture of a warden looking after a child. From the state of her clothes, it looks as though the girl has just been rescued from a bombed building.

Newspaper reports like the one below show how dangerous a warden's job could be.

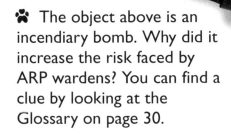

Dorset County Chronicle & Swanage Times
10 August 1939

IN CERTAIN areas men are unwilling to sign on as wardens on the ground that in ARP they run at least as much risk as special constables, and that 'specials' are paid whereas ARP volunteers are not. This is a misapprehension, as it is clearly laid down that except in a very few special cases, special constables are NOT paid.

❖ The object above is an incendiary bomb. Why did it increase the risk faced by ARP wardens? You can find a clue by looking at the Glossary on page 30.

Wardens carry an injured man to safety.

❖ Can you remember what the CD on these wardens' badges stands for?

Wardens organized first-aid posts and casualty-clearing stations, where people were looked after until ambulances arrived. On many occasions, wardens had to guide the ambulances, police and rescue parties to where they were needed. They also helped to fight fires until the fire brigade arrived.

DETECTIVE WORK

There may be someone in your family who can remember an air raid. Interview them about their experiences and ask permission to record their story on tape. They may even have been a warden during the war.

WARDENS—AFTER A RAID

The warden's role did not end when the raid ended. Wardens helped to clear debris from streets and other public places and dealt with buildings that were falling down. They also helped rescue parties to reach people who were trapped in buildings.

These rescue workers used a dog's keen sense of smell to find people trapped in collapsed buildings.

HOW TO GET HELP
after air raid damage

REST CENTRES provide temporary shelter for those whose houses are uninhabitable and who have not gone to friends or relatives

INJURY ALLOWANCES for persons of 15 years of age and over, medically certified incapable of work due to injuries sustained in air raids COMPENSATION: immediate help for immediate needs: loss of clothes, furniture, tools, etc., made good in certain circumstances	PAID THROUGH THE ASSISTANCE BOARD
PENSIONS for Widows and Dependent Relatives of workers and Civil Defence Volunteers who are killed or die from their injuries are granted in certain circumstances	PAID BY THE MINISTRY OF PENSIONS
DAMAGED HOUSES: first-aid repairs to make them wind and weather tight	DONE FREE BY THE LOCAL AUTHORITY
REMOVALS OR STORAGE of furniture from damaged houses RE-HOUSING & BILLETING of you and your family	HELP CAN BE GIVEN BY THE LOCAL AUTHORITY

LOST gas masks, identity cards, food ration books, unemployment insurance books, health insurance cards, pensions books, etc. are replaced

★ HELP AND INFORMATION ABOUT THESE SERVICES IS GIVEN AT THE INFORMATION CENTRE
ASK A POLICEMAN OR A.R.P. WARDEN FOR THE ADDRESS

This poster told people who had been bombed where they could seek help.

🐾 What do you think the R means on these workers' helmets?

Wardens were very important in getting life back to normal after an air raid. They were responsible for reporting all damage, and making sure that roads, sewers and water supplies were repaired as quickly as possible.

🐾 Look at the document on the left. How much did it cost for 'first aid' repairs to damaged houses?

Before the war started, as we have seen, wardens were trained to detect poison gas released by bombs, and to decontaminate affected areas. In fact, German bombers never dropped any bombs on Britain that contained gas.

In some areas, wardens carried out unusual tasks. Newspaper reports tell us that on the Isles of Scilly in January 1940, wardens had to use a boat to remove a body which had been washed up on a nearby island. In November 1939, the same wardens had to prevent farmers dropping seaweed when moving it from the beach to their fields. They were using it as fertilizer, but when they spilt the seaweed it made the roads slippery and dangerous.

The morning after a raid, when all the different tasks and the clearing up were finished, many tired wardens went off to work at their normal daytime jobs.

DETECTIVE WORK

Wardens had to write reports after an air raid. Sometimes these reports can be found in the Record Office, filed under 'Wartime, ARP'. They will refer to places damaged by bombs. Using this information, try to find a location which was bombed, and perhaps take a photograph of what the place looks like today. You may also be able to find out where the wardens' post was, and take a photograph of this location.

This warden was also a milkman, who had to start his milk round when he finished his warden's duties!

GAS MASKS

During the First World War, poison gas had been used as a weapon against troops. Many soldiers were killed as a result and some who survived had trouble breathing for the rest of their lives. The Government was afraid that during the Second World War, gas would be used against civilians.

This type of gas mask was issued to all adults and many children.

In October 1935, the Italian army invaded Abyssinia in Africa and used 'mustard gas' against civilians to force them out of their houses. Pictures of this action were shown in newspapers and on newsreels at cinemas in Britain. This made people realize that there was a real danger of gas attack.

A policeman in Fulham issues gas masks from the back of a lorry, in September 1938.

DORCHESTER GAS MASKS ISSUE

Gas Masks for the civilian population of Dorchester are being issued on **SUNDAY NEXT,** *August 27, from 9 a.m. to 9 p.m.*
The Masks will be issued from the various zone depots, details of which will be published in the "Echo" tomorrow night.

The Government decided to issue people with gas masks, which would allow them to breathe without being affected by gas. By 30 September 1938, 38 million gas masks had been issued. Local councils placed advertisements in newspapers, like the one on the left, telling people when they would be issued with their gas masks. You should be able to find these advertisements by looking through microfilm of your local newspapers from 1938–9.

Dorchester's *Daily Echo* newspaper from 26 August 1939.

❧ Why did people need to buy the following day's newspaper?

ARP committee minutes show that some places, such as Plymouth, did not get their masks until 1939. Local newspaper reports also show complaints from local people or officials who were not given the correct masks. The report below comes from the *Didcot Advertiser*, 21 October 1938.

A baby's respirator. The baby was placed inside and an adult used the pump to provide air.

Inside the respirator below is Neville Mooney, who was the first baby born in London after war was declared.

DIDCOT ADVERTISER
21 OCTOBER 1938

DIDCOT DID not receive the gas masks it needed. Out of 10,000 expected, 30% were large gas masks, 55% medium and only 15% were small which meant that it was the children who went without.

Special 'respirators' like those shown on the left were made for babies. But there was a shortage of these masks. The Treasury allowed the Government to buy 1.4 million of them at £1 each – but only on condition that they were issued at the very last minute!

DETECTIVE WORK

At the Record Office, look through the ARP committee minutes for your area for 1938–9. Try to find out when gas masks were first issued.

GAS-MASK DRILL

In schools there were gas-mask 'drills' or practices, where children wore their masks during lessons. This was not a very pleasant experience. Gas masks made your face very hot, and the smell of rubber made some people sick.

Children at the Kay Street Nursery School, Bolton, in 1940.

Masks for children were made with a red, rubber face-piece, blue container and bright eye-pieces. These became known as Mickey Mouse masks. Search the Record Office for letters about children's gas masks, like the one below.

> We find that existing gas masks are satisfactory and experiments that have been made in one or two day nurseries show that once the children get used to playing with them and see other children in them they lose their first fear of them.

Letter from the ARP department to the Marchioness of Reading, 11 May 1938

As the newspaper report below shows, some children thought of their gas masks as excellent toys.

A 'Mickey Mouse' gas mask, designed for younger children.

Boys Have Duels With Gas Masks At Weymouth

When Weymouth Education Committee yesterday discussed whether children in the town need always carry their respirators, reference was made to children 'slinging their gas masks about and having private duels with them'... Miss Sharp mentioned that several weeks ago she inspected a number of masks ... and found many filled with sand.

Dorset Daily Echo 30 November 1939

During the war people were encouraged to carry their gas masks at all times. Today, it is often thought that this was compulsory, but this was not actually the case. In fact, the Government relied on very good propaganda in advertisements and cinema films to persuade people to carry their masks.

A Gloucester policeman wears his gas mask to remind members of the public to carry their masks at all times.

Many posters told people to carry their gas masks.

Hitler will send **no warning –**

so always carry your gas mask

❂ What would the Government have used the pictures on this page for?

DETECTIVE WORK

Search through your local newspapers, and try to find advice given to people on how to look after their mask. Write down any instructions you find, like this: 'A thin film of toilet soap rubbed on the inside of the eye-piece will keep it from becoming misted by breath.'

BLACKOUT

During the hours of darkness, wardens made sure the 'blackout' was put into action. Any lights that might be seen from the air had to be put out, so German bombers could not see their targets. People were not even allowed to smoke cigarettes in the open.

WAIT FOR DAYLIGHT

the last hours of the **BLACKOUT** *are as important as the first*

This poster reminded people not to show lights early in the morning, before the blackout had finished.

DORSET CHRONICLE
AND SWANAGE TIMES
31 August 1939

PC CULTER saw the defendant light a match and then light cigarettes for the other men and then his own. He then deliberately held the match at arm's length and let it burn out. The Chairman considered this to be a very serious offence and the defendant was fined £3 and 7/6d costs. He would go to gaol for a month if the fine was not paid.

The blackout was first used on 1 September 1939. Can you imagine how much life changed at night for people who could use no lights in the street? The procedure was explained to people by sending them documents called ARP Circulars (numbers 223, 224, 226) which you might be able to find in your reference library or in the local Record Office.

These objects are luminous buttons, which people wore so that they could be seen in the blackout.

The man on the right is using a model clock to show people at what time their blackout curtains should be in place.

🐾 Do you think the photograph on the right was taken in summer or winter? There are three clues in the picture.

The blackout curtains in the hospital below have been painted with cartoons.

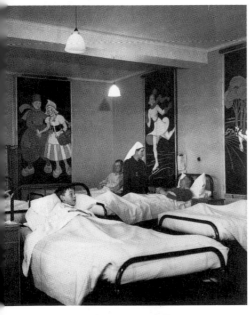

People had to put up blackout curtains at home, to stop light showing through their windows. Offices, factories and train carriages were blacked out. The hours when the blackout was in force were advertised in the local newspapers and displayed on signs.

Before the war started, there were blackout practices in many parts of the country. In 1938, RAF Whitley bombers pretended to attack Plymouth. Street lights were turned off and a large illuminated sign was used to ask the public to switch off their lights when they got home. Unfortunately, the pilots were still able to see the city because someone forgot to switch the sign off!

DETECTIVE WORK

When it is dark tonight, look out of your bedroom window. Write down all the things you see which use light. Now try to imagine what would happen if all those lights were turned off. This should help you to discover some of the problems caused by the blackout.

BLACKOUT ACCIDENTS

Various things were done to make life easier for people to find their way around during the blackout. Kerbstones and the bases of lamp-posts were painted white. Even some cows were painted with white stripes. So much white paint was used that there was a shortage, and the price went up.

Workers paint a lamp-post with white rings before the blackout begins.

Vehicles used masks like these to cover their lights.

❀ Why was the lamp-post above painted white?

Shops began advertising blackout items. Tape and paper were sold to help people black out their windows. Car headlights and traffic lights were fitted with masks which contained little cut-outs through which a small amount of light showed.

❀ What sort of vehicle used the covers on the left to black out its lights?

Some people called for the blackout to be ended, because they believed that it caused too many road accidents. But the blackout continued throughout the war. You may be able to track down some of the notices published in local newspapers by the Government, telling people to be careful in the dark.

This poster used the sharp eyes of a cat to tell people they should get used to the dark before starting to walk from a lit building.

UNTIL YOUR EYES GET USED TO THE DARKNESS, TAKE IT EASY

LOOK OUT IN THE BLACKOUT

GOVERNMENT NOTICE

Tonight on your way home there will be danger. Don't step off the kerb without looking both ways. Throw the light of your torch down on the ground so that you do not dazzle drivers. You cannot risk taking *any* chances.

Men were told to wear their white shirts hanging outside their trousers, so that they could be seen in the blackout. The Ministry of Food also told people that they should eat more carrots. The Vitamin A the carrots contained was supposed to help people see in the dark.

DETECTIVE WORK

Ask in your library to look at street directories. These have been published every year from the 1800s to the present day. Find a street directory from 1940, and look for shops advertising blackout material. Then look in the Yellow Pages to see if these shops still exist. If they do, you may be able to visit them and find out if they have any record of their wartime sales.

CROSS ONLY AT THE LIGHTS

Traffic lights had shields over them with small crosses showing the colours. This poster reminded people in the towns and cities to cross the road only at the traffic lights.

SHELTERS

When the air-raid siren sounded, people reacted in different ways. Some stayed at home. But many hurried through the darkness of the blackout to get to the safety of public shelters.

❀ These objects were used in air-raid shelters. What do you think they might be?

In Islington, London, people were issued with a card showing their details, the name of the public shelter they were allowed to use and the number of their bunk. On the back was the list of rules shown below.

❀ Read the document carefully. Who kept order in an air-raid shelter?
❀ How often were people expected to need the shelter?

READ THIS

This ticket may be withdrawn at the controller's discretion at any time and will be withdrawn if any of the following happen:

• The holder of this ticket or any member of his family ... creates any nuisance or disturbance in the shelter, or fails to do his share in keeping the shelter tidy and clean.

• This ticket is produced by someone other than the registered holder.

• The shelter is not used by the holder for four consecutive days without explanation.

• The holder disregards any lawful order or request of a police officer, air-raid wardens, shelter marshal, or other authorised marshal.

• The holder fails to remove from the shelter all bedding and personal belongings as and when required for cleaning purposes.

Many people built their own small shelters. Anderson shelters were made from sheets of corrugated iron and could house up to six people. They were dug into the garden and covered by soil, which some people used for growing vegetables. The shelters often flooded and the fire brigade had to pump them out.

DETECTIVE WORK

If your school was built before the war, you may find clues to where shelters were built in the playground. Over the years these may have changed into outside toilets or bicycle sheds. Take a camera and see if you can find one. Anderson shelters were very difficult to take apart, so some stayed in gardens and became garden sheds. You may also be able to track down one of these.

The picture above shows a family outside their Anderson shelter.

Anderson shelters were given free to anyone who earned under £250 a year. Over 2 million of them were built, and the Government sent out free pamphlets telling people how to make themselves comfortable in their shelters.

For those people who did not have a garden, there was the Morrison shelter. This was an iron-topped table with mesh sides. People could sleep under it inside their homes, and feel safe from falling debris.

Children asleep in a Morrison shelter.

THE UNDERGROUND

At the beginning of the Second World War, London Underground stations were not officially used as air-raid shelters, and were closed at night. This soon changed.

People sheltering in the Aldwych Tube Station, 8 October 1940.

The first Underground station to be opened as an official shelter was Aldwych (which closed down in 1993). Eventually 80 stations became shelters, for around 177,000 people. At first, the Underground shelters were very unhygienic. There were very few toilets so people had to relieve themselves in the tunnels. But conditions slowly improved.

☙ Read the article about the Underground in 1940. How many beds were available?

BLIGHTY MAGAZINE
23 December 1940

LONDON IS settling down to shelter life now, and 80,000 three-tier bunks have been delivered ... the London Tube system now has 134 canteens on the platforms, 60 electric boilers and ovens, with half a mile of specially installed water mains to serve them and a staff of 1,000. They sell 12,500 gallons of tea and cocoa every night, hot pies by the hundredweight and sausages by the quarter-mile.

George Formby was a film and musical star of the 1940s. Here he is entertaining people sheltering in Aldwych Station, by playing his ukelele.

DETECTIVE WORK

Read through some books about the Blitz, and write down the names of any Underground stations you find that were used as shelters. Here are the names of a few to start you off: Balham, Bank, Bethnal Green, Elephant and Castle, Trafalgar Square. Now find an A-Z mapbook of London at the library, and look at the map of the Underground on the back. Try to find your shelters on the map, and see whether or not they were all in one area. You can also use the map on the right, but it is an old document so it is harder to read.

When the bombing of London was at its most serious, people were queuing from as early as 11 am to get their place for the night. Some shelters were livened up with entertainment from well-known celebrities of the time, like the singer George Formby.

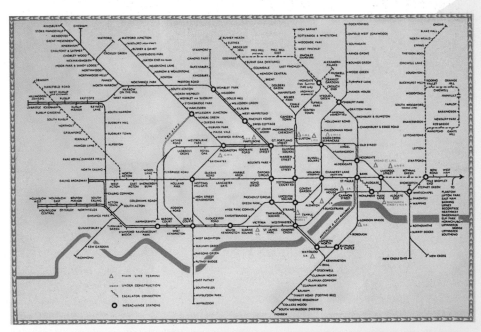

The map above was made during the Second World War. It shows you which stations were built, and could have been used as shelters.

🐾 Look closely at the map. What does a dotted line mean?

YOUR PROJECT

If you have been following the 'Detective Work' activities, you should now be able to track down enough clues to produce your own project looking at air raids in Britain during the Second World War.

First, you must decide on a topic to investigate. Choose one which interests you and is suitable for the area you live in. A good way to begin is to ask yourself a question. You can make up your own, or use one of the following suggestions.

Topic questions
- What were the responsibilities of local wardens?
- How did people obtain their gas masks?
- How did the blackout affect people's lives?
- What air-raid shelters were used in the local area?

This poster used a red traffic light and the red cross of first aid to tell people to cross the road carefully in the blackout.

During the war, horses were used to pull milk floats and bakers' vans. To protect them during a gas attack, councils issued gas protection bags. They had food at the bottom to keep the horse quiet.

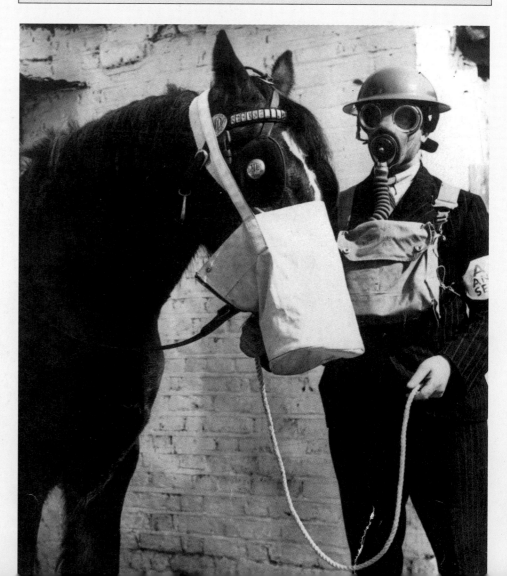

When you have found your information, it might make your project more interesting if you present it in an unusual way.

Project presentation
- Make your presentation in the form of a video documentary.
- Present your project as an 'archive' on computer.
- Write your project in the form of an air-raid warden's report.
- Collect all the cuttings and photographs you have found, and use them to make your own newspaper.
- Prepare an instruction manual for building an air-raid shelter.

You might find something unusual to study as your topic. Your project may throw some light on an accident in the blackout, or dig up some information about a hidden shelter. Sherlock has studied dogs, and found that even they wore gas masks.

The newspaper report below might help you to answer the question on page 5.

DORSET COUNTY CHRONICLE
31 AUGUST 1939

Remember that animals will not be permitted to enter public shelters. Of course, if you have a suitable private shelter, you should take them with you, but muzzle your dog and put your cat in a basket, for frenzied animals are dangerous and difficult to handle.

A dog fitted with its very own gas mask.
Do you think it could still bark?

GLOSSARY

ARP Air Raid Precautions (ARP) means both the group of workers who organized Britain's defence against air raids, and the measures they took.

casualty-clearing station A place where injured people were taken in order to see how serious their injuries were.

circulars Notices sent out to households by the Government.

Civil Defence (CD) An organization of civilians who were trained to protect people and property during the war.

civilians People not in the armed forces.

decontaminate Remove the effects of poison.

discretion One person's own judgement.

disregards Ignores, takes no notice of.

documents Pieces of written information that provide a record of an event.

evacuated Moved from areas of danger to areas which are thought to be safe.

incendiary bomb A bomb designed to cause fires.

microfilm Film on which pages from books, newspapers and documents are copied at a very small size, so they can be stored and read through a microfilm viewer.

mustard gas An oily liquid which causes painful blisters on the skin.

newsreels Films containing short news items which people watched in the cinema between the main feature films.

propaganda Written information, film, photographs or posters, which are used to put over a certain message or point of view.

respirator A gas mask.

shelter marshal Someone who was in charge of public shelters.

shrapnel Pieces of an exploded shell.

special constables Part-time policemen.

tear gas Gas which makes people's eyes water and sting.

Treasury The department which controls Government spending.

BOOKS TO READ
Non-fiction
Britain in World War II – The Blitz by Patricia Kendell (Wayland, 1998)
Home in the Blitz by Marilyn Tolhurst (A & C Black, 1996)
Johnnie's Blitz by Bernard Ashley (Viking, 1995)

Fiction
Harry's Battle of Britain by Andrew Donkin (Macdonald Young, 1999)
The Machine Gunners by Robert Westall (Nelson, 1996)

Children can use this book to improve their literacy skills in the following ways:

☑ To identify different types of text, and to understand the use of fact and opinion (Year 4, Term 1, Non-fiction reading comprehension).

☑ To identify the different purposes of ARP plans and instructions. (Year 3, Term 2, Non-fiction reading comprehension).

☑ To identify newspaper features, predict newspaper stories from headlines, and to write newspaper-style reports (Year 4, Term 1, Non-fiction reading comprehension and writing composition).

☑ To evaluate Government advertisements for their impact, appeal and honesty (Year 4, Term 3, Non-fiction reading comprehension).

PUZZLE ANSWERS

Page 5:

🐾 The strange object is an anti-gas kennel for dogs. Owners could put their dogs in one of these during a gas attack and they would be safe.

🐾 The gas-proof shoes were designed to be worn by farm animals, such as cows and sheep, to protect them from the effects of poison gas.

Page 6:

🐾 These badges were worn by members of the ARP, instructors who trained the wardens, and members of the Civil Defence (CD) who performed many ARP tasks.

Page 7:

🐾 The photograph was not taken in Glasgow, but in Fleet Street in London. You can see the address on the shop sign for Jack Hobbs Ltd, Sports Outfitters, 59 Fleet St.

🐾 She is holding her gas-mask case.

Page 9:

🐾 People were upset because ARP members might use their powers to boss their neighbours around and get even with people who had upset them before the war.

🐾 This famous recruiting poster was used to persuade men who were not already firemen to join the AFS or Auxiliary Fire Service. This service provided extra firemen during the war.

Page 10:

🐾 The poster makes the warden's job look glamorous and heroic, with its picture of the handsome warden and the word 'responsible' used twice.

Page 11:

🐾 The poster uses much simpler words. The slang phrase 'Arf a mo' is a short way of saying: 'Have you got half a moment to spare?'. The poster's simple language and funny cartoon try to appeal to a wide group of people.

Page 13

🐾 As the glossary says, an incendiary bomb – which contained chemicals – started fires when it exploded. Some incendiary bombs had timers in them so that they would explode later, often when rescue parties were in the area.

🐾 CD stands for Civil Defence.

Page 14:

🐾 The 'R' stands for Rescue.

🐾 The repairs were free.

Page 16:

🐾 The following day's newspaper contained details of 'zone depots' where gas masks could be collected.

Page 19:

🐾 The Government used photographs and posters like these to show people how important it was to carry their masks.

Page 21:

🐾 The photograph was taken in winter. The blackout starts at 4.40 pm and it only gets dark this early in winter. There are also no leaves on the trees in the background and the man is wearing an overcoat.

Page 22:

🐾 Lamp-posts were painted to help pedestrians and drivers see their way, and so that they would not drive into them.

🐾 These covers were used for cycle headlamps. You could be fined for not having covers on headlamps or for not having any headlamps at all.

Page 24:

🐾 The item on the left is a pump called a stirrup pump, used to put out small fires. You put the piece with the handle into a bucket of water, placed your foot on the flat piece on the right to keep it steady and pushed the handle up and down. The water then came out of the hose. The item on the right is a shelter lamp. It had a very small bulb with a magnifying glass in front of it to give more light.

🐾 Shelter marshals, wardens and the police kept order.

🐾 People were expected to use the shelters at least once every four nights. If they did not, their ticket was taken away.

Page 26:

🐾 240,000 beds were available (80,000 bunks, each with three 'tiers' or levels).

Page 27:

🐾 The key to the map explains that a dotted line shows an Underground line which is still under construction.

INDEX

Numbers in **bold** refer to pictures and captions.